50 Delicious Shake Recipes for Home

By: Kelly Johnson

Table of Contents

- Chocolate Peanut Butter Shake
- Vanilla Almond Protein Shake
- Strawberry Banana Shake
- Mango Pineapple Shake
- Blueberry Almond Shake
- Green Detox Shake
- Avocado Cilantro Lime Shake
- Classic Vanilla Shake
- Cookies and Cream Shake
- Berry Oatmeal Shake
- Pineapple Coconut Shake
- Kale Pineapple Shake
- Apple Cinnamon Shake
- Sweet Potato Pie Shake
- Greek Yogurt Pancake Batter Shake
- Easy Blender Salsa Shake
- Roasted Tomato Shake
- Cashew Cheese Sauce Shake
- Classic Guacamole Shake
- Cilantro Lime Rice Shake
- Vegan Alfredo Sauce Shake
- Smoothie Bowl Base Shake
- Vegan Creamy Caesar Dressing Shake
- Healthy Strawberry Shortcake Shake
- Spiced Pumpkin Shake
- Blackberry Chia Seed Shake
- Chocolate Avocado Pudding Shake
- Vegan Ice Cream Base Shake
- Mango Lassi Shake
- Beet Apple Shake
- Mint Chocolate Chip Shake
- Pineapple Mint Shake

- Creamy Avocado Cilantro Shake
- Sweet Green Shake
- Apple Ginger Shake
- Pear Spinach Shake
- Creamy Zucchini Shake
- Butternut Squash Shake
- Spicy Carrot Shake
- Vegan Creamy Mushroom Shake
- Chocolate Peanut Butter Milkshake
- Vanilla Almond Protein Shake
- Berry Oatmeal Shake
- Pineapple Coconut Shake
- Kale Pineapple Shake
- Apple Cinnamon Shake
- Sweet Potato Pie Shake
- Greek Yogurt Pancake Batter Shake
- Easy Blender Salsa Shake
- Roasted Tomato Sauce Shake

Chocolate Peanut Butter Shake

Ingredients:

- 1 cup milk of your choice (dairy, almond, soy, etc.)
- 1/2 cup Greek yogurt or non-dairy yogurt
- 2 tablespoons peanut butter (creamy or crunchy)
- 1 scoop chocolate protein powder (or 2 tablespoons cocoa powder)
- 1 banana (fresh or frozen)
- 1 tablespoon honey or maple syrup (optional, for extra sweetness)
- 1/2 cup ice cubes (optional, for a colder, thicker shake)

Instructions:

1. **Prepare Ingredients:**
   - If using a fresh banana, you can add ice cubes for a thicker shake. If using a frozen banana, you can skip the ice.
2. **Blend Ingredients:**
   - In a blender, combine the milk, Greek yogurt, peanut butter, chocolate protein powder (or cocoa powder), banana, and honey or maple syrup (if using).
3. **Blend Until Smooth:**
   - Blend on high until the mixture is smooth and creamy. If the shake is too thick, add a bit more milk to reach your desired consistency.
4. **Add Ice (Optional):**
   - If you're using fresh banana and want a colder, thicker shake, add a handful of ice cubes and blend again until smooth.
5. **Serve:**
   - Pour the shake into a glass and enjoy immediately.

Tips:

- **Peanut Butter:** For a richer flavor, use natural peanut butter. You can also substitute with almond butter or another nut butter.
- **Protein Powder:** Adjust the amount of protein powder based on your taste and dietary needs. If not using protein powder, you can add extra cocoa powder for a stronger chocolate flavor.
- **Sweetness:** Adjust the sweetness with honey or maple syrup as needed.

Enjoy your Chocolate Peanut Butter Shake!

Vanilla Almond Protein Shake

Ingredients:

- 1 cup milk of your choice (dairy, almond, soy, etc.)
- 1/2 cup Greek yogurt or non-dairy yogurt
- 1 scoop vanilla protein powder
- 1 tablespoon almond butter (or almond paste)
- 1/2 banana (fresh or frozen, for creaminess)
- 1 tablespoon honey or maple syrup (optional, for added sweetness)
- 1/2 teaspoon vanilla extract (optional, for extra vanilla flavor)
- 1/2 cup ice cubes (optional, for a colder, thicker shake)

Instructions:

1. **Prepare Ingredients:**
   - If using a fresh banana, you can add ice cubes for a thicker shake. If using a frozen banana, you can skip the ice.
2. **Blend Ingredients:**
   - In a blender, combine the milk, Greek yogurt, vanilla protein powder, almond butter, banana, and vanilla extract (if using).
3. **Blend Until Smooth:**
   - Blend on high until the mixture is smooth and creamy. If the shake is too thick, add a bit more milk to reach your desired consistency.
4. **Adjust Sweetness:**
   - Taste the shake and add honey or maple syrup if you prefer it sweeter. Blend again to combine.
5. **Add Ice (Optional):**
   - If using fresh banana and you want a colder, thicker shake, add a handful of ice cubes and blend again until smooth.
6. **Serve:**
   - Pour the shake into a glass and enjoy immediately.

Tips:

- **Almond Butter:** For a more intense almond flavor, use almond butter or almond paste. You can also substitute with other nut butters if desired.
- **Protein Powder:** Choose a vanilla-flavored protein powder for best results. Adjust the amount based on your taste and dietary needs.
- **Consistency:** Adjust the thickness by adding more milk if needed.

Enjoy your Vanilla Almond Protein Shake!

Strawberry Banana Shake

Ingredients:

- 1 cup fresh or frozen strawberries (hulled)
- 1 banana (fresh or frozen)
- 1/2 cup Greek yogurt or non-dairy yogurt
- 1/2 cup milk of your choice (dairy, almond, soy, etc.)
- 1 tablespoon honey or maple syrup (optional, for added sweetness)
- 1/2 teaspoon vanilla extract (optional, for extra flavor)
- 1/2 cup ice cubes (optional, for a colder, thicker shake)

Instructions:

1. **Prepare Ingredients:**
   - If using fresh strawberries, you may want to add ice cubes for a thicker shake. If using frozen strawberries, you can skip the ice.
2. **Blend Ingredients:**
   - In a blender, combine the strawberries, banana, Greek yogurt, milk, and vanilla extract (if using).
3. **Blend Until Smooth:**
   - Blend on high until the mixture is smooth and creamy. If the shake is too thick, add a bit more milk to reach your desired consistency.
4. **Adjust Sweetness:**
   - Taste the shake and add honey or maple syrup if you prefer it sweeter. Blend again to combine.
5. **Add Ice (Optional):**
   - If using fresh strawberries and you want a colder, thicker shake, add a handful of ice cubes and blend again until smooth.
6. **Serve:**
   - Pour the shake into a glass and enjoy immediately.

Tips:

- **Strawberries:** Use ripe strawberries for the best flavor. If using frozen strawberries, the shake will be thicker and colder.
- **Banana:** A ripe banana will add natural sweetness and creaminess. Using a frozen banana will make the shake even creamier.
- **Yogurt:** Greek yogurt adds creaminess and a bit of protein. You can use non-dairy yogurt if you prefer a dairy-free option.

Enjoy your refreshing Strawberry Banana Shake!

Mango Pineapple Shake

Ingredients:

- 1 cup fresh or frozen mango chunks
- 1 cup fresh or frozen pineapple chunks
- 1/2 cup Greek yogurt or non-dairy yogurt
- 1/2 cup coconut water or any milk of your choice
- 1 tablespoon honey or maple syrup (optional, for added sweetness)
- 1/2 teaspoon vanilla extract (optional, for extra flavor)
- 1/2 cup ice cubes (optional, for a colder, thicker shake)

Instructions:

1. **Prepare Ingredients:**
   - If using fresh mango and pineapple, you can add ice cubes to make the shake colder and thicker. If using frozen fruit, you can skip the ice.
2. **Blend Ingredients:**
   - In a blender, combine the mango chunks, pineapple chunks, Greek yogurt, coconut water (or milk), and vanilla extract (if using).
3. **Blend Until Smooth:**
   - Blend on high until the mixture is smooth and creamy. If the shake is too thick, add a bit more coconut water or milk to reach your desired consistency.
4. **Adjust Sweetness:**
   - Taste the shake and add honey or maple syrup if you prefer it sweeter. Blend again to combine.
5. **Add Ice (Optional):**
   - If using fresh fruit and you want a colder, thicker shake, add a handful of ice cubes and blend again until smooth.
6. **Serve:**
   - Pour the shake into a glass and enjoy immediately.

Tips:

- **Fruit:** Using frozen mango and pineapple makes the shake colder and thicker, while fresh fruit will give it a lighter texture.
- **Coconut Water:** Coconut water adds a subtle tropical flavor and extra hydration, but you can substitute with any milk of your choice.
- **Sweetness:** Adjust sweetness according to your preference. Tropical fruits are usually sweet enough, but you can add a bit more honey or syrup if needed.

Enjoy your tropical Mango Pineapple Shake!

Blueberry Almond Shake

Ingredients:

- 1 cup fresh or frozen blueberries
- 1/2 banana (fresh or frozen, for creaminess)
- 1 cup milk of your choice (dairy, almond, soy, etc.)
- 2 tablespoons almond butter (or almond paste)
- 1/2 cup Greek yogurt or non-dairy yogurt
- 1 tablespoon honey or maple syrup (optional, for added sweetness)
- 1/4 teaspoon vanilla extract (optional, for extra flavor)
- 1/2 cup ice cubes (optional, for a colder, thicker shake)

Instructions:

1. **Prepare Ingredients:**
   - If using fresh blueberries and banana, you might want to add ice cubes for a thicker shake. If using frozen blueberries and banana, you can skip the ice.
2. **Blend Ingredients:**
   - In a blender, combine the blueberries, banana, milk, almond butter, Greek yogurt, and vanilla extract (if using).
3. **Blend Until Smooth:**
   - Blend on high until the mixture is smooth and creamy. If the shake is too thick, add a bit more milk to reach your desired consistency.
4. **Adjust Sweetness:**
   - Taste the shake and add honey or maple syrup if you prefer it sweeter. Blend again to combine.
5. **Add Ice (Optional):**
   - If using fresh fruit and you want a colder, thicker shake, add a handful of ice cubes and blend again until smooth.
6. **Serve:**
   - Pour the shake into a glass and enjoy immediately.

Tips:

- **Blueberries:** Fresh or frozen blueberries work well. Frozen blueberries will make the shake thicker and colder.
- **Almond Butter:** For a richer almond flavor, use almond butter. You can also substitute with other nut butters if desired.
- **Creaminess:** Greek yogurt adds creaminess and extra protein. Use non-dairy yogurt for a dairy-free option.

Enjoy your nutritious and tasty Blueberry Almond Shake!

Green Detox Shake

Ingredients:

- 1 cup fresh spinach or kale leaves (stems removed)
- 1/2 green apple, cored and chopped
- 1/2 cucumber, peeled and chopped
- 1/2 banana (fresh or frozen, for creaminess)
- 1/2 cup Greek yogurt or non-dairy yogurt
- 1 cup unsweetened almond milk or any milk of your choice
- 1 tablespoon lemon juice (about 1/2 lemon)
- 1 tablespoon honey or maple syrup (optional, for added sweetness)
- 1/2 cup ice cubes (optional, for a colder, thicker shake)

Instructions:

1. **Prepare Ingredients:**
   - If using a fresh banana, you can add ice cubes to make the shake colder and thicker. If using a frozen banana, you can skip the ice.
2. **Blend Ingredients:**
   - In a blender, combine the spinach or kale, green apple, cucumber, banana, Greek yogurt, almond milk, and lemon juice.
3. **Blend Until Smooth:**
   - Blend on high until the mixture is smooth and creamy. If the shake is too thick, add a bit more almond milk to reach your desired consistency.
4. **Adjust Sweetness:**
   - Taste the shake and add honey or maple syrup if you prefer it sweeter. Blend again to combine.
5. **Add Ice (Optional):**
   - If using fresh fruit and you want a colder, thicker shake, add a handful of ice cubes and blend again until smooth.
6. **Serve:**
   - Pour the shake into a glass and enjoy immediately.

Tips:

- **Greens:** Spinach has a milder flavor than kale, making it a good choice for those new to green smoothies. Kale has a slightly more robust flavor.
- **Apple:** Use a tart green apple like Granny Smith for a refreshing kick.
- **Cucumber:** Adds a light, hydrating flavor and helps with the shake's consistency.
- **Creaminess:** Greek yogurt adds creaminess and protein. You can use non-dairy yogurt for a dairy-free option.

Enjoy your revitalizing Green Detox Shake!

Avocado Cilantro Lime Shake

Ingredients:

- 1 ripe avocado
- 1/2 cup fresh cilantro leaves (packed)
- 1/2 cup Greek yogurt or non-dairy yogurt
- 1 cup unsweetened almond milk or any milk of your choice
- Juice of 1 lime (about 2 tablespoons)
- 1 tablespoon honey or maple syrup (optional, for added sweetness)
- 1/2 cup ice cubes (optional, for a colder, thicker shake)
- Optional: 1/2 banana (for extra creaminess)

Instructions:

1. **Prepare Ingredients:**
   - Cut the avocado in half, remove the pit, and scoop the flesh into a blender.
   - Rinse and pat dry the cilantro leaves.
   - If using a fresh banana, add ice cubes for a thicker shake. If using a frozen banana, you can skip the ice.
2. **Blend Ingredients:**
   - In a blender, combine the avocado, cilantro, Greek yogurt, almond milk, lime juice, and honey or maple syrup (if using).
3. **Blend Until Smooth:**
   - Blend on high until the mixture is smooth and creamy. If the shake is too thick, add a bit more almond milk to reach your desired consistency.
4. **Add Ice (Optional):**
   - If you're using fresh ingredients and want a colder, thicker shake, add a handful of ice cubes and blend again until smooth.
5. **Serve:**
   - Pour the shake into a glass and enjoy immediately.

Tips:

- **Avocado:** Use a ripe avocado for the best creaminess and flavor.
- **Cilantro:** Cilantro adds a fresh, herbaceous flavor. If you're not a fan of cilantro, you can substitute parsley.
- **Sweetness:** Adjust the sweetness with honey or maple syrup according to your taste preferences.
- **Creaminess:** Adding a banana will make the shake even creamier, but it's optional.

Enjoy your creamy and refreshing Avocado Cilantro Lime Shake!

Classic Vanilla Shake
Ingredients:

- 1 cup vanilla ice cream
- 1/2 cup milk of your choice (dairy, almond, soy, etc.)
- 1/2 teaspoon vanilla extract
- Whipped cream (optional, for topping)
- Maraschino cherry (optional, for garnish)

Instructions:

1. **Blend Ingredients:**
    - In a blender, combine the vanilla ice cream, milk, and vanilla extract.
2. **Blend Until Smooth:**
    - Blend on high until the mixture is smooth and creamy. If the shake is too thick, add a little more milk to reach your desired consistency.
3. **Serve:**
    - Pour the shake into a glass.
4. **Add Toppings (Optional):**
    - Top with whipped cream and a maraschino cherry, if desired.
5. **Enjoy:**
    - Serve immediately with a straw or a spoon.

Tips:

- **Ice Cream:** For a richer flavor, use high-quality vanilla ice cream.
- **Milk:** Adjust the amount of milk based on your preferred thickness. Less milk will make the shake thicker, while more milk will make it thinner.
- **Vanilla Extract:** Adds an extra layer of vanilla flavor, but you can omit it if you prefer a purer vanilla taste.

Enjoy your classic and delicious Vanilla Shake!

Cookies and Cream Shake

Ingredients:

- 4-6 Oreo cookies (or any chocolate sandwich cookies)
- 1 cup vanilla ice cream
- 1/2 cup milk of your choice (dairy, almond, soy, etc.)
- 1/2 cup Greek yogurt or non-dairy yogurt (optional, for extra creaminess)
- Whipped cream (optional, for topping)
- Extra crushed cookies (optional, for garnish)

Instructions:

1. **Prepare Cookies:**
   - Crush the Oreo cookies into smaller pieces. You can do this by placing them in a plastic bag and crushing them with a rolling pin or using a food processor.
2. **Blend Ingredients:**
   - In a blender, combine the crushed cookies, vanilla ice cream, milk, and Greek yogurt (if using).
3. **Blend Until Smooth:**
   - Blend on high until the mixture is smooth and creamy, with chunks of cookie throughout. If the shake is too thick, add a little more milk to reach your desired consistency.
4. **Serve:**
   - Pour the shake into a glass.
5. **Add Toppings (Optional):**
   - Top with whipped cream and sprinkle extra crushed cookies on top for added texture and flavor.
6. **Enjoy:**
   - Serve immediately with a straw or a spoon.

Tips:

- **Cookies:** Use your favorite brand of chocolate sandwich cookies. The more cookies you add, the chunkier the shake will be.
- **Ice Cream:** For a richer shake, use high-quality vanilla ice cream.
- **Creaminess:** Greek yogurt adds extra creaminess and a bit of protein, but you can omit it if you prefer a classic shake.

Enjoy your indulgent Cookies and Cream Shake!

Berry Oatmeal Shake

Ingredients:

- 1 cup mixed berries (fresh or frozen, such as strawberries, blueberries, raspberries, and blackberries)
- 1/2 cup rolled oats
- 1/2 banana (fresh or frozen, for creaminess)
- 1 cup milk of your choice (dairy, almond, soy, etc.)
- 1/2 cup Greek yogurt or non-dairy yogurt
- 1 tablespoon honey or maple syrup (optional, for added sweetness)
- 1/2 teaspoon vanilla extract (optional, for extra flavor)
- 1/2 cup ice cubes (optional, for a colder, thicker shake)

Instructions:

1. **Prepare Ingredients:**
   - If using fresh berries and banana, you can add ice cubes for a thicker shake. If using frozen berries and banana, you can skip the ice.
2. **Blend Ingredients:**
   - In a blender, combine the mixed berries, rolled oats, banana, milk, Greek yogurt, and vanilla extract (if using).
3. **Blend Until Smooth:**
   - Blend on high until the mixture is smooth and creamy. If the shake is too thick, add a bit more milk to reach your desired consistency.
4. **Adjust Sweetness:**
   - Taste the shake and add honey or maple syrup if you prefer it sweeter. Blend again to combine.
5. **Add Ice (Optional):**
   - If using fresh ingredients and you want a colder, thicker shake, add a handful of ice cubes and blend again until smooth.
6. **Serve:**
   - Pour the shake into a glass and enjoy immediately.

Tips:

- **Berries:** Using a mix of berries adds a variety of flavors and nutrients. Frozen berries will make the shake colder and thicker.
- **Oats:** Rolled oats blend well into the shake and add fiber. For a smoother texture, you can blend the oats separately with the milk before adding the other ingredients.
- **Creaminess:** Greek yogurt adds creaminess and protein. You can use non-dairy yogurt for a dairy-free option.

Enjoy your nutritious and delicious Berry Oatmeal Shake!

Pineapple Coconut Shake

Ingredients:

- 1 cup fresh or frozen pineapple chunks
- 1/2 cup coconut milk (full-fat or light, based on your preference)
- 1/2 cup Greek yogurt or non-dairy yogurt
- 1 tablespoon coconut flakes or shredded coconut (optional, for added texture)
- 1 tablespoon honey or maple syrup (optional, for added sweetness)
- 1/2 teaspoon vanilla extract (optional, for extra flavor)
- 1/2 cup ice cubes (optional, for a colder, thicker shake)

Instructions:

1. **Prepare Ingredients:**
    - If using fresh pineapple, you might want to add ice cubes to make the shake colder and thicker. If using frozen pineapple, you can skip the ice.
2. **Blend Ingredients:**
    - In a blender, combine the pineapple chunks, coconut milk, Greek yogurt, coconut flakes (if using), and vanilla extract (if using).
3. **Blend Until Smooth:**
    - Blend on high until the mixture is smooth and creamy. If the shake is too thick, add a bit more coconut milk to reach your desired consistency.
4. **Adjust Sweetness:**
    - Taste the shake and add honey or maple syrup if you prefer it sweeter. Blend again to combine.
5. **Add Ice (Optional):**
    - If using fresh pineapple and you want a colder, thicker shake, add a handful of ice cubes and blend again until smooth.
6. **Serve:**
    - Pour the shake into a glass and enjoy immediately.

Tips:

- **Pineapple:** Fresh pineapple provides a bright, tangy flavor. Frozen pineapple will make the shake thicker and colder.
- **Coconut Milk:** For a richer taste, use full-fat coconut milk. Light coconut milk works if you prefer a lighter option.
- **Coconut Flakes:** Adding shredded coconut gives the shake extra texture and a more pronounced coconut flavor.

Enjoy your tropical Pineapple Coconut Shake!

Kale Pineapple Shake

Ingredients:

- 1 cup fresh kale leaves (stems removed)
- 1 cup fresh or frozen pineapple chunks
- 1/2 banana (fresh or frozen, for creaminess)
- 1 cup unsweetened almond milk or any milk of your choice
- 1/2 cup Greek yogurt or non-dairy yogurt
- 1 tablespoon honey or maple syrup (optional, for added sweetness)
- 1/2 teaspoon vanilla extract (optional, for extra flavor)
- 1/2 cup ice cubes (optional, for a colder, thicker shake)

Instructions:

1. **Prepare Ingredients:**
    - If using fresh pineapple and banana, you might want to add ice cubes for a thicker shake. If using frozen pineapple and banana, you can skip the ice.
2. **Blend Ingredients:**
    - In a blender, combine the kale leaves, pineapple chunks, banana, almond milk, Greek yogurt, and vanilla extract (if using).
3. **Blend Until Smooth:**
    - Blend on high until the mixture is smooth and creamy. If the shake is too thick, add a bit more almond milk to reach your desired consistency.
4. **Adjust Sweetness:**
    - Taste the shake and add honey or maple syrup if you prefer it sweeter. Blend again to combine.
5. **Add Ice (Optional):**
    - If using fresh fruit and you want a colder, thicker shake, add a handful of ice cubes and blend again until smooth.
6. **Serve:**
    - Pour the shake into a glass and enjoy immediately.

Tips:

- **Kale:** Fresh kale is the best option. Make sure to remove the tough stems before blending.
- **Pineapple:** Using frozen pineapple will give the shake a thicker texture and colder temperature.
- **Banana:** A ripe banana adds natural sweetness and creaminess. Frozen banana will enhance the shake's thickness.

Enjoy your nutritious and delicious Kale Pineapple Shake!

Apple Cinnamon Shake

Ingredients:

- 1 medium apple (cored and chopped, skin on or off as preferred)
- 1/2 teaspoon ground cinnamon
- 1/2 cup Greek yogurt or non-dairy yogurt
- 1 cup milk of your choice (dairy, almond, soy, etc.)
- 1 tablespoon honey or maple syrup (optional, for added sweetness)
- 1/2 teaspoon vanilla extract (optional, for extra flavor)
- 1/2 cup ice cubes (optional, for a colder, thicker shake)

Instructions:

1. **Prepare Ingredients:**
   - Core and chop the apple. If you prefer, you can peel the apple, though keeping the skin on adds extra fiber.
   - If using a fresh apple, you might want to add ice cubes for a thicker shake. If using a frozen apple, you can skip the ice.
2. **Blend Ingredients:**
   - In a blender, combine the chopped apple, ground cinnamon, Greek yogurt, milk, and vanilla extract (if using).
3. **Blend Until Smooth:**
   - Blend on high until the mixture is smooth and creamy. If the shake is too thick, add a bit more milk to reach your desired consistency.
4. **Adjust Sweetness:**
   - Taste the shake and add honey or maple syrup if you prefer it sweeter. Blend again to combine.
5. **Add Ice (Optional):**
   - If using fresh apple and you want a colder, thicker shake, add a handful of ice cubes and blend again until smooth.
6. **Serve:**
   - Pour the shake into a glass and enjoy immediately.

Tips:

- **Apples:** Use a sweet apple like Fuji or Gala for a naturally sweeter shake. For a bit of tartness, you can use Granny Smith apples.
- **Cinnamon:** Adjust the amount of ground cinnamon to your taste preference. You can also sprinkle a little extra cinnamon on top for garnish.
- **Creaminess:** Greek yogurt adds creaminess and a bit of protein. You can use non-dairy yogurt for a dairy-free option.

Enjoy your comforting and flavorful Apple Cinnamon Shake!

Sweet Potato Pie Shake

Ingredients:

- 1 cup cooked and mashed sweet potato (about 1 medium sweet potato, peeled and cooked)
- 1/2 cup vanilla ice cream or non-dairy ice cream
- 1/2 cup milk of your choice (dairy, almond, soy, etc.)
- 1/4 teaspoon ground cinnamon
- 1/4 teaspoon ground nutmeg
- 1/4 teaspoon vanilla extract
- 1 tablespoon maple syrup or honey (optional, for added sweetness)
- 1/2 cup ice cubes (optional, for a colder, thicker shake)
- Whipped cream (optional, for topping)
- Extra ground cinnamon or nutmeg (optional, for garnish)

Instructions:

1. **Prepare Sweet Potato:**
   - Peel and cook the sweet potato until tender. You can boil, steam, or bake it. Once cooked, mash it until smooth and let it cool slightly.
2. **Blend Ingredients:**
   - In a blender, combine the mashed sweet potato, vanilla ice cream, milk, ground cinnamon, ground nutmeg, vanilla extract, and maple syrup or honey (if using).
3. **Blend Until Smooth:**
   - Blend on high until the mixture is smooth and creamy. If the shake is too thick, add a bit more milk to reach your desired consistency.
4. **Add Ice (Optional):**
   - If using fresh ingredients and you want a colder, thicker shake, add a handful of ice cubes and blend again until smooth.
5. **Serve:**
   - Pour the shake into a glass.
6. **Add Toppings (Optional):**
   - Top with whipped cream and sprinkle extra ground cinnamon or nutmeg on top for a festive touch.
7. **Enjoy:**
   - Serve immediately with a straw or a spoon.

Tips:

- **Sweet Potato:** Make sure the sweet potato is well-mashed and smooth to blend easily. You can use canned sweet potato puree if you prefer a quicker option.
- **Ice Cream:** Vanilla ice cream adds creaminess and complements the sweet potato flavor. Use non-dairy ice cream for a dairy-free option.

- **Spices:** Adjust the spices to your taste. You can also add a pinch of ground ginger for extra warmth.

Enjoy your delicious and comforting Sweet Potato Pie Shake!

Greek Yogurt Pancake Batter Shake

Ingredients:

- 1 cup Greek yogurt (plain or vanilla)
- 1/2 cup milk of your choice (dairy, almond, soy, etc.)
- 1/2 cup rolled oats
- 1 tablespoon honey or maple syrup (for added sweetness)
- 1/2 teaspoon vanilla extract
- 1/2 teaspoon ground cinnamon
- 1/4 teaspoon baking powder (for a fluffier texture)
- 1/2 banana (fresh or frozen, for creaminess)
- 1/2 cup ice cubes (optional, for a colder, thicker shake)

Instructions:

1. **Prepare Ingredients:**
   - If using fresh banana and you want a thicker, colder shake, you might want to add ice cubes. If using a frozen banana, you can skip the ice.
2. **Blend Ingredients:**
   - In a blender, combine the Greek yogurt, milk, rolled oats, honey or maple syrup, vanilla extract, ground cinnamon, baking powder, and banana.
3. **Blend Until Smooth:**
   - Blend on high until the mixture is smooth and creamy. The oats should be fully blended into the shake. If it's too thick, add a bit more milk to reach your desired consistency.
4. **Add Ice (Optional):**
   - If you want a colder, thicker shake and you're using fresh ingredients, add a handful of ice cubes and blend again until smooth.
5. **Serve:**
   - Pour the shake into a glass.
6. **Enjoy:**
   - Serve immediately and enjoy your pancake-inspired shake!

Tips:

- **Oats:** Rolled oats blend well into the shake and provide a subtle pancake flavor. For a smoother texture, you can blend the oats with the milk first before adding other ingredients.
- **Greek Yogurt:** Use plain Greek yogurt for a tangy flavor or vanilla Greek yogurt for added sweetness.
- **Sweetness:** Adjust the sweetness with honey or maple syrup based on your preference.

Enjoy your Greek Yogurt Pancake Batter Shake, a delightful and healthy twist on traditional pancakes!

Easy Blender Salsa Shake

Ingredients:

- 1 cup salsa (store-bought or homemade, mild or spicy based on your preference)
- 1/2 cup Greek yogurt or non-dairy yogurt (for creaminess)
- 1/2 cup milk of your choice (dairy, almond, soy, etc.)
- 1/4 cup fresh cilantro leaves
- 1/4 teaspoon ground cumin
- 1/4 teaspoon garlic powder
- 1/4 teaspoon onion powder
- 1 tablespoon lime juice (about 1/2 lime)
- 1/2 avocado (for added creaminess, optional)
- 1/2 cup ice cubes (optional, for a colder, thicker shake)

Instructions:

1. **Prepare Ingredients:**
   - If using fresh salsa and you want a thicker, colder shake, add ice cubes. If using store-bought salsa, you can skip the ice if you prefer.
2. **Blend Ingredients:**
   - In a blender, combine the salsa, Greek yogurt, milk, cilantro, ground cumin, garlic powder, onion powder, lime juice, and avocado (if using).
3. **Blend Until Smooth:**
   - Blend on high until the mixture is smooth and creamy. If the shake is too thick, add a bit more milk to reach your desired consistency.
4. **Add Ice (Optional):**
   - If using fresh salsa and you want a colder, thicker shake, add a handful of ice cubes and blend again until smooth.
5. **Serve:**
   - Pour the shake into a glass.
6. **Enjoy:**
   - Serve immediately for a refreshing and savory twist!

Tips:

- **Salsa:** Use your favorite salsa, whether mild, medium, or hot. Fresh salsa will give a fresher taste, while store-bought salsa can add more consistency.
- **Creaminess:** Greek yogurt adds creaminess and a bit of tang. You can use non-dairy yogurt for a dairy-free version.
- **Flavor Balance:** Adjust the spices and lime juice to balance the flavors according to your taste preference.

Enjoy your savory and unique Easy Blender Salsa Shake!

Roasted Tomato Shake

Ingredients:

- 2 cups roasted tomatoes (about 4-6 medium tomatoes, roasted)
- 1/2 cup Greek yogurt or non-dairy yogurt
- 1/2 cup milk of your choice (dairy, almond, soy, etc.)
- 1/4 cup fresh basil leaves (or a handful of fresh herbs like parsley or cilantro)
- 1 tablespoon lemon juice (about 1/2 lemon)
- 1/4 teaspoon garlic powder
- 1/4 teaspoon onion powder
- Salt and pepper to taste
- 1/2 cup ice cubes (optional, for a colder, thicker shake)

Instructions:

1. **Roast Tomatoes:**
    - Preheat your oven to 400°F (200°C). Cut the tomatoes in half and place them on a baking sheet. Drizzle with olive oil, and season with salt and pepper. Roast for 20-25 minutes or until the tomatoes are soft and slightly caramelized. Allow them to cool before using.
2. **Prepare Ingredients:**
    - Once the roasted tomatoes are cool, scoop them into a blender. If using fresh tomatoes, you may want to add a bit of olive oil to mimic the richness of roasted tomatoes.
3. **Blend Ingredients:**
    - In the blender, combine the roasted tomatoes, Greek yogurt, milk, fresh basil leaves, lemon juice, garlic powder, and onion powder.
4. **Blend Until Smooth:**
    - Blend on high until the mixture is smooth and creamy. If the shake is too thick, add a bit more milk to reach your desired consistency.
5. **Add Ice (Optional):**
    - If you want a colder, thicker shake and you're using fresh roasted tomatoes, add a handful of ice cubes and blend again until smooth.
6. **Season to Taste:**
    - Taste the shake and adjust the seasoning with salt and pepper as needed.
7. **Serve:**
    - Pour the shake into a glass.
8. **Enjoy:**
    - Serve immediately for a refreshing and savory twist!

Tips:

- **Roasted Tomatoes:** Roasting intensifies the tomato flavor and adds a slightly sweet, caramelized touch. If you prefer, you can use store-bought roasted tomatoes or sun-dried tomatoes.
- **Creaminess:** Greek yogurt adds creaminess and a tangy flavor. Non-dairy yogurt can be used for a dairy-free option.
- **Fresh Herbs:** Fresh basil or other herbs add a vibrant flavor. You can also use dried herbs if fresh herbs are not available.

Enjoy your unique and savory Roasted Tomato Shake!

Cashew Cheese Sauce Shake

Ingredients:

- 1 cup cashew cheese sauce (homemade or store-bought, see recipe below)
- 1/2 cup milk of your choice (dairy, almond, soy, etc.)
- 1/2 cup Greek yogurt or non-dairy yogurt
- 1 tablespoon lemon juice (about 1/2 lemon)
- 1/2 teaspoon garlic powder
- 1/4 teaspoon onion powder
- Salt and pepper to taste
- 1/2 cup ice cubes (optional, for a colder, thicker shake)

For Homemade Cashew Cheese Sauce:

- 1 cup raw cashews, soaked for 2-4 hours (or overnight) and drained
- 1/2 cup water
- 1/4 cup nutritional yeast
- 1 tablespoon lemon juice
- 1 clove garlic
- 1/2 teaspoon paprika
- Salt to taste

Instructions:

1. **Prepare Cashew Cheese Sauce:**
    - In a blender or food processor, combine the soaked and drained cashews, water, nutritional yeast, lemon juice, garlic, paprika, and a pinch of salt.
    - Blend until smooth and creamy. Adjust the seasoning to taste. If the sauce is too thick, add a little more water to achieve your desired consistency.
2. **Blend Shake Ingredients:**
    - In a blender, combine 1 cup of the cashew cheese sauce, milk, Greek yogurt, lemon juice, garlic powder, and onion powder.
3. **Blend Until Smooth:**
    - Blend on high until the mixture is smooth and well combined. If the shake is too thick, add a bit more milk to reach your desired consistency.
4. **Add Ice (Optional):**
    - If using fresh ingredients and you want a colder, thicker shake, add a handful of ice cubes and blend again until smooth.
5. **Season to Taste:**
    - Taste the shake and adjust the seasoning with salt and pepper as needed.
6. **Serve:**
    - Pour the shake into a glass.
7. **Enjoy:**

- Serve immediately for a unique and savory shake experience!

Tips:

- **Cashew Cheese Sauce:** You can use store-bought cashew cheese sauce if you prefer convenience. Homemade cashew cheese sauce can be customized to your taste by adjusting the seasoning.
- **Creaminess:** Greek yogurt adds extra creaminess. You can use non-dairy yogurt for a dairy-free version.
- **Seasoning:** Adjust the seasoning and spices according to your preference. You might also add a dash of hot sauce for extra flavor.

Enjoy your savory and creamy Cashew Cheese Sauce Shake!

Classic Guacamole Shake

Ingredients:

- 1 ripe avocado
- 1/2 cup Greek yogurt or non-dairy yogurt (for creaminess)
- 1/2 cup milk of your choice (dairy, almond, soy, etc.)
- 1/4 cup fresh cilantro leaves
- 1 tablespoon lime juice (about 1/2 lime)
- 1 small garlic clove
- 1/4 teaspoon ground cumin
- 1/4 teaspoon onion powder
- Salt and pepper to taste
- 1/2 cup ice cubes (optional, for a colder, thicker shake)

Instructions:

1. **Prepare Ingredients:**
   - Scoop out the flesh of the avocado and place it in a blender.
   - If you want a colder shake, you can add ice cubes.
2. **Blend Ingredients:**
   - In a blender, combine the avocado, Greek yogurt, milk, fresh cilantro, lime juice, garlic clove, ground cumin, and onion powder.
3. **Blend Until Smooth:**
   - Blend on high until the mixture is smooth and creamy. If the shake is too thick, add a bit more milk to reach your desired consistency.
4. **Season to Taste:**
   - Taste the shake and adjust the seasoning with salt and pepper as needed. You can also add more lime juice for extra tanginess.
5. **Add Ice (Optional):**
   - If you're using fresh ingredients and prefer a colder, thicker shake, add a handful of ice cubes and blend again until smooth.
6. **Serve:**
   - Pour the shake into a glass.
7. **Enjoy:**
   - Serve immediately for a refreshing and savory twist on traditional guacamole!

Tips:

- **Avocado:** Use a ripe avocado for the best creamy texture. If you have leftover guacamole, you can also use it, but adjust the seasoning as needed.
- **Greek Yogurt:** Adds creaminess and a slight tang. Non-dairy yogurt can be used for a dairy-free option.

- **Cilantro:** Fresh cilantro adds a bright, herbal flavor. You can also use parsley or omit if you prefer a different flavor profile.

Enjoy your savory and creamy Classic Guacamole Shake!

Cilantro Lime Rice Shake

Ingredients:

- 1/2 cup cooked white or brown rice (cooled)
- 1/2 cup Greek yogurt or non-dairy yogurt (for creaminess)
- 1/2 cup milk of your choice (dairy, almond, soy, etc.)
- 1/4 cup fresh cilantro leaves
- 1 tablespoon lime juice (about 1/2 lime)
- 1/4 teaspoon ground cumin
- 1/4 teaspoon garlic powder
- Salt and pepper to taste
- 1/2 cup ice cubes (optional, for a colder, thicker shake)

Instructions:

1. **Prepare Rice:**
    - If you haven't already, cook and cool the rice before using it. This recipe works well with both white and brown rice.
2. **Blend Ingredients:**
    - In a blender, combine the cooked rice, Greek yogurt, milk, fresh cilantro, lime juice, ground cumin, and garlic powder.
3. **Blend Until Smooth:**
    - Blend on high until the mixture is smooth and creamy. If the shake is too thick, add a bit more milk to reach your desired consistency.
4. **Season to Taste:**
    - Taste the shake and adjust the seasoning with salt and pepper as needed.
5. **Add Ice (Optional):**
    - If using fresh ingredients and you want a colder, thicker shake, add a handful of ice cubes and blend again until smooth.
6. **Serve:**
    - Pour the shake into a glass.
7. **Enjoy:**
    - Serve immediately for a refreshing and savory shake experience!

Tips:

- **Rice:** Make sure the rice is fully cooked and cooled before blending. You can use leftover rice if it's available.
- **Greek Yogurt:** Adds creaminess and a slight tang. Non-dairy yogurt can be used for a dairy-free option.
- **Cilantro:** Fresh cilantro gives the shake a vibrant, herbaceous flavor. You can also use parsley if you prefer a different herb.

Enjoy your unique and refreshing Cilantro Lime Rice Shake!

Vegan Alfredo Sauce Shake

Ingredients:

- 1 cup vegan Alfredo sauce (homemade or store-bought, see recipe below)
- 1/2 cup unsweetened almond milk or any plant-based milk
- 1/2 cup silken tofu or cashew cream (for extra creaminess)
- 1 tablespoon nutritional yeast (for a cheesy flavor)
- 1 tablespoon lemon juice (about 1/2 lemon)
- 1/4 teaspoon garlic powder
- 1/4 teaspoon onion powder
- Salt and pepper to taste
- 1/2 cup ice cubes (optional, for a colder, thicker shake)

For Homemade Vegan Alfredo Sauce:

- 1 cup raw cashews (soaked for at least 2 hours or overnight)
- 1 cup water
- 1/4 cup nutritional yeast
- 1 tablespoon lemon juice
- 1 clove garlic
- 1/4 teaspoon onion powder
- 1/4 teaspoon ground nutmeg
- Salt to taste

Instructions:

1. **Prepare Vegan Alfredo Sauce:**
   - If making homemade vegan Alfredo sauce, drain and rinse the soaked cashews. In a blender, combine the cashews, water, nutritional yeast, lemon juice, garlic, onion powder, nutmeg, and a pinch of salt. Blend until smooth and creamy. Adjust seasoning to taste.
2. **Blend Shake Ingredients:**
   - In a blender, combine 1 cup of the vegan Alfredo sauce, almond milk, silken tofu or cashew cream, nutritional yeast, lemon juice, garlic powder, and onion powder.
3. **Blend Until Smooth:**
   - Blend on high until the mixture is smooth and well combined. If the shake is too thick, add a bit more almond milk to reach your desired consistency.
4. **Add Ice (Optional):**
   - If you want a colder, thicker shake and you're using fresh ingredients, add a handful of ice cubes and blend again until smooth.
5. **Season to Taste:**
   - Taste the shake and adjust the seasoning with salt and pepper as needed.
6. **Serve:**

    - Pour the shake into a glass.
7. **Enjoy:**
    - Serve immediately for a savory and creamy shake experience!

Tips:

- **Alfredo Sauce:** Store-bought vegan Alfredo sauce can be used for convenience, but homemade sauce allows you to control the flavor and texture.
- **Creaminess:** Silken tofu or cashew cream adds extra creaminess. Adjust the amount based on your desired consistency.
- **Nutritional Yeast:** Adds a cheesy flavor to the shake. Adjust according to taste.

Enjoy your innovative and delicious Vegan Alfredo Sauce Shake!

Smoothie Bowl Base Shake

Ingredients:

- 1 cup frozen fruit (e.g., berries, mango, banana, or a mix)
- 1/2 cup Greek yogurt or non-dairy yogurt
- 1/2 cup milk of your choice (dairy, almond, soy, etc.)
- 1 tablespoon honey or maple syrup (optional, for added sweetness)
- 1 tablespoon chia seeds or flaxseeds (optional, for added texture and nutrition)
- 1/4 teaspoon vanilla extract (optional, for extra flavor)
- 1/2 cup ice cubes (optional, for a thicker, colder shake)

Instructions:

1. **Prepare Ingredients:**
   - If using fresh fruit, you may want to add ice cubes for a thicker texture. If using frozen fruit, you can skip the ice.
2. **Blend Ingredients:**
   - In a blender, combine the frozen fruit, Greek yogurt, milk, honey or maple syrup (if using), chia seeds or flaxseeds (if using), and vanilla extract (if using).
3. **Blend Until Smooth:**
   - Blend on high until the mixture is smooth and creamy. If the shake is too thick, add a bit more milk to achieve your desired consistency.
4. **Add Ice (Optional):**
   - If using fresh fruit and you prefer a thicker, colder shake, add a handful of ice cubes and blend again until smooth.
5. **Serve:**
   - Pour the shake into a bowl.
6. **Customize:**
   - Top with your favorite toppings like fresh fruit slices, granola, nuts, seeds, coconut flakes, or a drizzle of honey.
7. **Enjoy:**
   - Enjoy immediately as a delicious and nutritious smoothie bowl!

Tips:

- **Fruit:** Choose your favorite frozen fruit for the base. Bananas add natural sweetness and creaminess, while berries or mangoes provide a vibrant flavor.
- **Greek Yogurt:** Adds creaminess and a bit of protein. Non-dairy yogurt can be used for a dairy-free option.
- **Toppings:** Customize with various toppings to add texture and extra nutrients. Fresh fruit, granola, and seeds are great choices.

Enjoy your versatile and customizable Smoothie Bowl Base Shake!

Vegan Creamy Caesar Dressing Shake

Ingredients:

- 1 cup vegan Caesar dressing (store-bought or homemade, see recipe below)
- 1/2 cup unsweetened almond milk or any plant-based milk
- 1/2 cup silken tofu or non-dairy yogurt (for extra creaminess)
- 1 tablespoon nutritional yeast (for a cheesy flavor)
- 1 tablespoon lemon juice (about 1/2 lemon)
- 1 clove garlic (or 1/2 teaspoon garlic powder)
- 1 teaspoon Dijon mustard
- 1/4 teaspoon onion powder
- Salt and pepper to taste
- 1/2 cup ice cubes (optional, for a colder, thicker shake)

For Homemade Vegan Caesar Dressing:

- 1/2 cup raw cashews (soaked for at least 2 hours or overnight and drained)
- 1/4 cup water
- 2 tablespoons lemon juice
- 2 tablespoons nutritional yeast
- 1 tablespoon Dijon mustard
- 1 clove garlic
- 1 tablespoon capers (drained)
- 1 tablespoon tamari or soy sauce
- Salt and pepper to taste

Instructions:

1. **Prepare Vegan Caesar Dressing:**
   - In a blender, combine the soaked and drained cashews, water, lemon juice, nutritional yeast, Dijon mustard, garlic, capers, and tamari or soy sauce.
   - Blend until smooth and creamy. Adjust the seasoning with salt and pepper. If the dressing is too thick, add a little more water.
2. **Blend Shake Ingredients:**
   - In a blender, combine 1 cup of the vegan Caesar dressing, almond milk, silken tofu or non-dairy yogurt, nutritional yeast, lemon juice, garlic, Dijon mustard, and onion powder.
3. **Blend Until Smooth:**
   - Blend on high until the mixture is smooth and creamy. If the shake is too thick, add a bit more almond milk to reach your desired consistency.
4. **Add Ice (Optional):**
   - If using fresh ingredients and you want a colder, thicker shake, add a handful of ice cubes and blend again until smooth.

5. **Season to Taste:**
   - Taste the shake and adjust the seasoning with salt and pepper as needed.
6. **Serve:**
   - Pour the shake into a glass or use it as a dip.
7. **Enjoy:**
   - Serve immediately for a unique and savory shake experience!

Tips:

- **Vegan Caesar Dressing:** Store-bought vegan Caesar dressing can be used for convenience. Homemade dressing allows you to control the flavor and consistency.
- **Creaminess:** Silken tofu or non-dairy yogurt adds extra creaminess. Adjust the amount based on your desired consistency.
- **Seasoning:** Adjust the spices and flavorings to taste. You can add a dash of hot sauce or extra nutritional yeast for more flavor.

Enjoy your savory and creamy Vegan Creamy Caesar Dressing Shake!

Healthy Strawberry Shortcake Shake

Ingredients:

- 1 cup frozen strawberries (or fresh strawberries if you prefer a less thick texture)
- 1/2 cup Greek yogurt or non-dairy yogurt (for creaminess)
- 1/2 cup milk of your choice (dairy, almond, soy, etc.)
- 1 tablespoon honey or maple syrup (optional, for added sweetness)
- 1/4 cup rolled oats (for a shortcake-like texture)
- 1/2 teaspoon vanilla extract
- 1/4 teaspoon ground cinnamon (optional, for a touch of spice)
- 1/2 banana (for natural sweetness and creaminess, optional)
- 1/2 cup ice cubes (optional, for a thicker, colder shake)

Instructions:

1. **Prepare Ingredients:**
   - If using fresh strawberries, you might want to add ice cubes to achieve a thicker consistency. If using frozen strawberries, you can skip the ice.
2. **Blend Ingredients:**
   - In a blender, combine the frozen strawberries, Greek yogurt, milk, rolled oats, honey or maple syrup (if using), vanilla extract, and ground cinnamon (if using).
3. **Blend Until Smooth:**
   - Blend on high until the mixture is smooth and creamy. The rolled oats will blend into the shake, providing a texture reminiscent of shortcake. If the shake is too thick, add a bit more milk to reach your desired consistency.
4. **Add Banana (Optional):**
   - For extra creaminess and sweetness, add the banana to the blender and blend until fully combined.
5. **Add Ice (Optional):**
   - If you're using fresh strawberries and want a thicker, colder shake, add a handful of ice cubes and blend again until smooth.
6. **Serve:**
   - Pour the shake into a glass.
7. **Enjoy:**
   - Serve immediately for a refreshing and healthy treat!

Tips:

- **Strawberries:** Fresh or frozen strawberries work well. Frozen strawberries give the shake a thicker texture.
- **Oats:** Rolled oats add a shortcake-like texture and a bit of heartiness. They also help thicken the shake.

- **Sweetness:** Adjust the sweetness with honey or maple syrup based on your preference. The banana adds natural sweetness if you choose to use it.
- **Flavor:** Ground cinnamon adds a nice touch of spice, but you can leave it out if you prefer.

Enjoy your Healthy Strawberry Shortcake Shake!

Spiced Pumpkin Shake

Ingredients:

- 1 cup canned pumpkin puree (not pumpkin pie filling)
- 1/2 cup Greek yogurt or non-dairy yogurt
- 1/2 cup milk of your choice (dairy, almond, soy, etc.)
- 1 tablespoon maple syrup or honey (optional, for added sweetness)
- 1/2 teaspoon vanilla extract
- 1/2 teaspoon ground cinnamon
- 1/4 teaspoon ground nutmeg
- 1/4 teaspoon ground ginger
- Pinch of ground cloves (optional)
- 1/2 banana (for added creaminess, optional)
- 1/2 cup ice cubes (optional, for a colder, thicker shake)

Instructions:

1. **Prepare Ingredients:**
   - If you're using fresh pumpkin or a less thick milk, you might want to add ice cubes to thicken the shake. If using canned pumpkin, no need for ice unless you prefer a colder texture.
2. **Blend Ingredients:**
   - In a blender, combine the canned pumpkin puree, Greek yogurt, milk, maple syrup or honey (if using), vanilla extract, ground cinnamon, nutmeg, ginger, and cloves (if using).
3. **Blend Until Smooth:**
   - Blend on high until the mixture is smooth and creamy. The banana can be added here if you want extra creaminess and natural sweetness.
4. **Add Ice (Optional):**
   - If you're using fresh pumpkin or want a thicker, colder shake, add a handful of ice cubes and blend again until smooth.
5. **Serve:**
   - Pour the shake into a glass.
6. **Enjoy:**
   - Serve immediately for a refreshing and spiced treat!

Tips:

- **Pumpkin Puree:** Use canned pumpkin puree for convenience. If using fresh pumpkin, roast or steam and blend until smooth before adding to the shake.
- **Sweetness:** Adjust the sweetness with maple syrup or honey according to your taste preference. The banana also adds natural sweetness if used.

- **Spices:** Adjust the spices to taste. You can use pumpkin pie spice blend in place of individual spices if you prefer.

Enjoy your flavorful and comforting Spiced Pumpkin Shake!

Blackberry Chia Seed Shake

Ingredients:

- 1 cup fresh or frozen blackberries
- 1/2 cup Greek yogurt or non-dairy yogurt
- 1/2 cup milk of your choice (dairy, almond, soy, etc.)
- 1 tablespoon chia seeds
- 1 tablespoon honey or maple syrup (optional, for added sweetness)
- 1/2 teaspoon vanilla extract (optional, for extra flavor)
- 1/2 banana (for added creaminess, optional)
- 1/2 cup ice cubes (optional, for a thicker, colder shake)

Instructions:

1. **Prepare Chia Seeds:**
   - If using dry chia seeds, let them sit in a small bowl with 2 tablespoons of water for about 10-15 minutes to absorb the liquid and swell. This will give them a gel-like texture. If you prefer, you can also blend them directly into the shake.
2. **Blend Ingredients:**
   - In a blender, combine the blackberries, Greek yogurt, milk, chia seeds (pre-soaked or dry), honey or maple syrup (if using), and vanilla extract (if using).
3. **Blend Until Smooth:**
   - Blend on high until the mixture is smooth and creamy. If you're using a banana, add it to the blender for extra creaminess and sweetness.
4. **Add Ice (Optional):**
   - If using fresh blackberries and you want a colder, thicker shake, add a handful of ice cubes and blend again until smooth.
5. **Serve:**
   - Pour the shake into a glass.
6. **Enjoy:**
   - Serve immediately for a refreshing and nutritious shake!

Tips:

- **Blackberries:** Fresh or frozen blackberries work well. Frozen blackberries will make the shake thicker and colder.
- **Chia Seeds:** Soaking chia seeds helps to create a gel-like texture. You can blend them directly if you prefer a smoother shake.
- **Sweetness:** Adjust the sweetness with honey or maple syrup to taste. The banana adds natural sweetness if you use it.

Enjoy your tasty and nutritious Blackberry Chia Seed Shake!

Chocolate Avocado Pudding Shake

Ingredients:

- 1 ripe avocado
- 2 tablespoons unsweetened cocoa powder
- 2 tablespoons maple syrup or honey (or to taste)
- 1/2 cup Greek yogurt or non-dairy yogurt
- 1/2 cup milk of your choice (dairy, almond, soy, etc.)
- 1/2 teaspoon vanilla extract
- Pinch of salt
- 1/2 cup ice cubes (optional, for a colder, thicker shake)

Instructions:

1. **Prepare Avocado:**
   - Cut the avocado in half, remove the pit, and scoop the flesh into the blender.
2. **Blend Ingredients:**
   - In a blender, combine the avocado, unsweetened cocoa powder, maple syrup or honey, Greek yogurt, milk, vanilla extract, and a pinch of salt.
3. **Blend Until Smooth:**
   - Blend on high until the mixture is completely smooth and creamy. If you prefer a thinner consistency, you can add a bit more milk.
4. **Add Ice (Optional):**
   - If you're using fresh avocado and want a colder, thicker shake, add a handful of ice cubes and blend again until smooth.
5. **Serve:**
   - Pour the shake into a glass.
6. **Enjoy:**
   - Serve immediately for a rich and creamy treat!

Tips:

- **Avocado:** Ensure the avocado is ripe for the best creamy texture. If it's overripe, the flavor might be off.
- **Sweetness:** Adjust the sweetness with maple syrup or honey according to your taste preference.
- **Consistency:** The shake can be adjusted for thickness by adding more or less milk. Ice can also make it thicker and colder.

Enjoy your delicious and creamy Chocolate Avocado Pudding Shake!

Vegan Ice Cream Base Shake

Ingredients:

- 1 cup canned coconut milk (full-fat for creaminess) or any plant-based milk
- 1/2 cup cashews (soaked for at least 2 hours or overnight and drained)
- 1/2 cup non-dairy yogurt (plain or vanilla)
- 1/4 cup maple syrup or agave syrup (or to taste)
- 1 tablespoon vanilla extract
- 1/4 teaspoon salt
- 1/2 cup ice cubes (optional, for a colder, thicker shake)

Instructions:

1. **Prepare Cashews:**
    - Soak the cashews in water for at least 2 hours or overnight to soften. Drain and rinse before using.
2. **Blend Ingredients:**
    - In a blender, combine the soaked cashews, coconut milk, non-dairy yogurt, maple syrup or agave syrup, vanilla extract, and salt.
3. **Blend Until Smooth:**
    - Blend on high until the mixture is completely smooth and creamy. The cashews should blend into a smooth texture, providing a creamy consistency.
4. **Add Ice (Optional):**
    - If you want a colder, thicker shake, add a handful of ice cubes and blend again until smooth.
5. **Serve:**
    - Pour the shake into a glass or use it as a base for creating different ice cream flavors.
6. **Customize:**
    - To turn this base into various ice cream flavors, add mix-ins or flavorings such as fruit purées, cocoa powder, spices, or extracts. Blend until combined and freeze according to your chosen method.

Tips:

- **Cashews:** Ensure cashews are soaked well to achieve a smooth texture. They help create a creamy base for the ice cream.
- **Coconut Milk:** Full-fat coconut milk adds richness. If you prefer a lighter base, use a lower-fat plant-based milk but expect a less creamy result.
- **Sweetener:** Adjust the amount of maple syrup or agave syrup based on your desired sweetness level.

Enjoy your versatile Vegan Ice Cream Base Shake! Feel free to experiment with different flavors and add-ins to create your favorite vegan ice cream treats.

Mango Lassi Shake

Ingredients:

- 1 cup fresh or frozen mango chunks (if using frozen, you might want to add less ice)
- 1/2 cup Greek yogurt or non-dairy yogurt
- 1/2 cup milk of your choice (dairy, almond, soy, etc.)
- 2 tablespoons honey or maple syrup (or to taste)
- 1/4 teaspoon ground cardamom (optional, for traditional flavor)
- 1/4 teaspoon vanilla extract (optional, for added flavor)
- 1/2 teaspoon lemon juice (optional, for a hint of tartness)
- 1/2 cup ice cubes (optional, for a colder, thicker shake)

Instructions:

1. **Prepare Ingredients:**
   - If using fresh mangoes, you may want to add ice cubes to thicken the shake. If using frozen mangoes, you can skip the ice.
2. **Blend Ingredients:**
   - In a blender, combine the mango chunks, Greek yogurt, milk, honey or maple syrup, ground cardamom (if using), vanilla extract (if using), and lemon juice (if using).
3. **Blend Until Smooth:**
   - Blend on high until the mixture is smooth and creamy. Adjust the sweetness with honey or maple syrup according to your taste.
4. **Add Ice (Optional):**
   - If you're using fresh mangoes and want a thicker, colder shake, add a handful of ice cubes and blend again until smooth.
5. **Serve:**
   - Pour the shake into a glass.
6. **Enjoy:**
   - Serve immediately for a refreshing and creamy treat!

Tips:

- **Mango:** Use ripe mangoes for the best flavor. Frozen mangoes can make the shake colder and thicker.
- **Yogurt:** Greek yogurt adds creaminess and a bit of tang. Non-dairy yogurt can be used for a dairy-free option.
- **Cardamom:** Adds a traditional touch to the lassi. If you don't have cardamom, you can omit it or use a pinch of cinnamon as an alternative.
- **Sweetness:** Adjust sweetness with honey or maple syrup based on your preference.

Enjoy your delicious Mango Lassi Shake!

Beet Apple Shake

Ingredients:

- 1 small cooked beet (peeled and chopped) or 1/2 cup pre-cooked beet cubes
- 1 medium apple, cored and chopped
- 1/2 cup Greek yogurt or non-dairy yogurt
- 1/2 cup milk of your choice (dairy, almond, soy, etc.)
- 1 tablespoon honey or maple syrup (or to taste)
- 1/2 teaspoon vanilla extract (optional, for added flavor)
- 1/2 teaspoon ground cinnamon (optional, for extra warmth)
- 1/2 cup ice cubes (optional, for a colder, thicker shake)

Instructions:

1. **Prepare Beets:**
   - If using raw beets, peel and chop them, then steam or roast until tender. If using pre-cooked beet cubes, they're ready to use.
2. **Prepare Ingredients:**
   - Core and chop the apple. If you prefer a colder shake, you can chill the apple beforehand or add ice.
3. **Blend Ingredients:**
   - In a blender, combine the cooked beet, apple, Greek yogurt, milk, honey or maple syrup, and vanilla extract (if using). Add the ground cinnamon if desired.
4. **Blend Until Smooth:**
   - Blend on high until the mixture is smooth and creamy. Adjust sweetness to taste with additional honey or maple syrup if needed.
5. **Add Ice (Optional):**
   - If you want a thicker, colder shake and you're using fresh ingredients, add a handful of ice cubes and blend again until smooth.
6. **Serve:**
   - Pour the shake into a glass.
7. **Enjoy:**
   - Serve immediately for a refreshing and nutritious treat!

Tips:

- **Beets:** Cooking beets beforehand helps to soften them and enhance their natural sweetness. Pre-cooked beet cubes can be found in grocery stores for convenience.
- **Apple:** Use a crisp apple variety for the best flavor. Adjust the apple type based on your taste preference.
- **Yogurt:** Greek yogurt adds creaminess and a bit of tang. Non-dairy yogurt can be used for a dairy-free option.

- **Sweetness:** Adjust the sweetness with honey or maple syrup according to your preference.

Enjoy your nutritious and delicious Beet Apple Shake!

Mint Chocolate Chip Shake

Ingredients:

- 1 cup milk of your choice (dairy, almond, soy, etc.)
- 1/2 cup Greek yogurt or non-dairy yogurt
- 1/4 cup fresh mint leaves (or 1/2 teaspoon peppermint extract)
- 1/4 cup chocolate chips (dark or semi-sweet)
- 1 tablespoon honey or maple syrup (or to taste)
- 1/2 teaspoon vanilla extract (optional, for extra flavor)
- 1/2 cup ice cubes (optional, for a colder, thicker shake)

Instructions:

1. **Prepare Mint:**
   - If using fresh mint leaves, lightly crush them to release more flavor.
2. **Blend Ingredients:**
   - In a blender, combine the milk, Greek yogurt, fresh mint leaves (or peppermint extract), chocolate chips, honey or maple syrup, and vanilla extract (if using).
3. **Blend Until Smooth:**
   - Blend on high until the mixture is smooth and the mint and chocolate chips are well combined. The mint leaves should be finely blended into the shake.
4. **Add Ice (Optional):**
   - If you prefer a thicker, colder shake, add a handful of ice cubes and blend again until smooth.
5. **Serve:**
   - Pour the shake into a glass.
6. **Enjoy:**
   - Serve immediately for a refreshing and creamy treat!

Tips:

- **Mint:** If using peppermint extract instead of fresh mint, start with a small amount and adjust to taste. Peppermint extract is quite strong, so a little goes a long way.
- **Chocolate Chips:** You can use mini chocolate chips for a better texture or chop larger chips if you prefer.
- **Sweetness:** Adjust the sweetness with honey or maple syrup according to your taste.

Enjoy your cool and indulgent Mint Chocolate Chip Shake!

Pineapple Mint Shake

Ingredients:

- 1 cup fresh or frozen pineapple chunks
- 1/2 cup Greek yogurt or non-dairy yogurt
- 1/2 cup milk of your choice (dairy, almond, soy, etc.)
- 1/4 cup fresh mint leaves (or 1/2 teaspoon mint extract)
- 1 tablespoon honey or maple syrup (or to taste)
- 1/2 teaspoon lime juice (optional, for extra tang)
- 1/2 cup ice cubes (optional, for a thicker, colder shake)

Instructions:

1. **Prepare Mint:**
    - If using fresh mint leaves, lightly crush them to release more flavor.
2. **Blend Ingredients:**
    - In a blender, combine the pineapple chunks, Greek yogurt, milk, fresh mint leaves (or mint extract), honey or maple syrup, and lime juice (if using).
3. **Blend Until Smooth:**
    - Blend on high until the mixture is smooth and the mint is well incorporated. If using fresh mint, make sure it's finely blended into the shake.
4. **Add Ice (Optional):**
    - If you're using fresh pineapple and prefer a thicker, colder shake, add a handful of ice cubes and blend again until smooth.
5. **Serve:**
    - Pour the shake into a glass.
6. **Enjoy:**
    - Serve immediately for a refreshing and tropical treat!

Tips:

- **Pineapple:** Use ripe pineapple for the best flavor. Frozen pineapple chunks can make the shake colder and thicker.
- **Mint:** If using mint extract instead of fresh mint, start with a small amount and adjust to taste. Mint extract is quite concentrated.
- **Sweetness:** Adjust the sweetness with honey or maple syrup according to your taste preference.
- **Lime Juice:** Adds a nice tangy contrast to the sweetness of the pineapple. Omit if you prefer a sweeter shake.

Enjoy your tropical Pineapple Mint Shake!

Creamy Avocado Cilantro Shake

Ingredients:

- 1 ripe avocado
- 1/2 cup Greek yogurt or non-dairy yogurt
- 1/2 cup milk of your choice (dairy, almond, soy, etc.)
- 1/4 cup fresh cilantro leaves
- 1 tablespoon lime juice (about half a lime)
- 1 tablespoon honey or maple syrup (or to taste)
- 1/2 teaspoon ground cumin (optional, for a hint of spice)
- 1/2 cup ice cubes (optional, for a colder, thicker shake)

Instructions:

1. **Prepare Avocado:**
   - Cut the avocado in half, remove the pit, and scoop the flesh into the blender.
2. **Blend Ingredients:**
   - In a blender, combine the avocado, Greek yogurt, milk, fresh cilantro leaves, lime juice, honey or maple syrup, and ground cumin (if using).
3. **Blend Until Smooth:**
   - Blend on high until the mixture is smooth and creamy. The avocado will provide a rich texture, and the cilantro will infuse the shake with fresh flavor.
4. **Add Ice (Optional):**
   - If you prefer a thicker, colder shake, add a handful of ice cubes and blend again until smooth.
5. **Serve:**
   - Pour the shake into a glass.
6. **Enjoy:**
   - Serve immediately for a creamy and refreshing treat!

Tips:

- **Avocado:** Ensure the avocado is ripe for the best creamy texture. Overripe avocados might have an off flavor.
- **Cilantro:** Fresh cilantro adds a vibrant flavor. Adjust the amount according to your taste preference. If you're not a fan of cilantro, you can substitute with fresh mint for a different flavor profile.
- **Sweetness:** Adjust the sweetness with honey or maple syrup based on your preference.
- **Cumin:** Ground cumin adds a hint of spice and depth. You can omit it if you prefer a simpler flavor.

Enjoy your unique and creamy Avocado Cilantro Shake!

Sweet Green Shake

Ingredients:

- 1 cup spinach leaves (fresh or frozen)
- 1/2 cup kale leaves, stems removed
- 1 ripe banana
- 1/2 cup green apple, cored and chopped
- 1/2 cup pineapple chunks (fresh or frozen)
- 1/2 cup Greek yogurt or non-dairy yogurt
- 1/2 cup milk of your choice (dairy, almond, soy, etc.)
- 1 tablespoon honey or maple syrup (or to taste)
- 1 tablespoon chia seeds (optional, for added nutrition)
- 1/2 cup ice cubes (optional, for a colder, thicker shake)

Instructions:

1. **Prepare Ingredients:**
    - If using fresh spinach and kale, wash them thoroughly. Chop the apple and pineapple into chunks. Peel the banana.
2. **Blend Ingredients:**
    - In a blender, combine the spinach, kale, banana, green apple, pineapple, Greek yogurt, milk, and honey or maple syrup.
3. **Blend Until Smooth:**
    - Blend on high until the mixture is completely smooth and creamy. The spinach and kale should be finely blended into the shake.
4. **Add Ice (Optional):**
    - If you prefer a thicker, colder shake, add a handful of ice cubes and blend again until smooth.
5. **Add Chia Seeds (Optional):**
    - If using chia seeds, blend them in with the other ingredients. They will add a bit of texture and extra nutrients.
6. **Serve:**
    - Pour the shake into a glass.
7. **Enjoy:**
    - Serve immediately for a refreshing and nutrient-packed treat!

Tips:

- **Greens:** Spinach and kale are both great sources of vitamins and minerals. If you're new to green shakes, start with more spinach and less kale, as kale has a stronger flavor.
- **Sweetness:** Adjust the sweetness with honey or maple syrup according to your taste. The banana and pineapple also contribute natural sweetness.

- **Milk:** Use any milk of your choice to achieve the desired consistency. Plant-based milks like almond or coconut milk work well for a lighter option.

Enjoy your healthy and delicious Sweet Green Shake!

Apple Ginger Shake

Ingredients:

- 1 medium apple, cored and chopped
- 1/2 teaspoon fresh ginger, peeled and grated (or 1/4 teaspoon ground ginger)
- 1/2 cup Greek yogurt or non-dairy yogurt
- 1/2 cup milk of your choice (dairy, almond, soy, etc.)
- 1 tablespoon honey or maple syrup (or to taste)
- 1/2 teaspoon vanilla extract (optional, for added flavor)
- 1/2 cup ice cubes (optional, for a colder, thicker shake)
- 1/4 teaspoon cinnamon (optional, for extra warmth)

Instructions:

1. **Prepare Ingredients:**
    - Core and chop the apple. Peel and grate the fresh ginger. If you prefer a colder shake, you might want to add ice.
2. **Blend Ingredients:**
    - In a blender, combine the chopped apple, grated ginger, Greek yogurt, milk, honey or maple syrup, and vanilla extract (if using).
3. **Blend Until Smooth:**
    - Blend on high until the mixture is smooth and creamy. Make sure the ginger is well incorporated into the shake.
4. **Add Ice (Optional):**
    - If you want a thicker, colder shake and you're using fresh apple, add a handful of ice cubes and blend again until smooth.
5. **Add Cinnamon (Optional):**
    - For an extra touch of warmth, you can blend in 1/4 teaspoon of ground cinnamon.
6. **Serve:**
    - Pour the shake into a glass.
7. **Enjoy:**
    - Serve immediately for a fresh and invigorating treat!

Tips:

- **Apple:** Use a crisp apple variety for the best flavor. Adjust the type based on your preference for sweetness or tartness.
- **Ginger:** Fresh ginger provides a sharper flavor compared to ground ginger. Adjust the amount based on your taste preference.
- **Sweetness:** Adjust the sweetness with honey or maple syrup based on your taste. The apple also adds natural sweetness.
- **Milk:** Use your preferred milk to achieve the desired consistency.

Enjoy your refreshing and flavorful Apple Ginger Shake!

Pear Spinach Shake

Ingredients:

- 1 ripe pear, cored and chopped
- 1 cup fresh spinach leaves (packed)
- 1/2 cup Greek yogurt or non-dairy yogurt
- 1/2 cup milk of your choice (dairy, almond, soy, etc.)
- 1 tablespoon honey or maple syrup (or to taste)
- 1/2 teaspoon vanilla extract (optional, for added flavor)
- 1/2 teaspoon lemon juice (optional, for a hint of tang)
- 1/2 cup ice cubes (optional, for a colder, thicker shake)

Instructions:

1. **Prepare Ingredients:**
   - Core and chop the pear. Wash the spinach thoroughly. If you prefer a colder shake, you might want to add ice.
2. **Blend Ingredients:**
   - In a blender, combine the chopped pear, spinach leaves, Greek yogurt, milk, honey or maple syrup, and vanilla extract (if using).
3. **Blend Until Smooth:**
   - Blend on high until the mixture is smooth and creamy. The spinach will blend into the shake, giving it a vibrant green color.
4. **Add Lemon Juice (Optional):**
   - For a hint of tang and to enhance the flavors, add 1/2 teaspoon of lemon juice.
5. **Add Ice (Optional):**
   - If using fresh pear and you want a thicker, colder shake, add a handful of ice cubes and blend again until smooth.
6. **Serve:**
   - Pour the shake into a glass.
7. **Enjoy:**
   - Serve immediately for a refreshing and nutritious treat!

Tips:

- **Pear:** Use a ripe pear for natural sweetness and a smooth texture. Adjust the type based on your taste preference.
- **Spinach:** Fresh spinach is used here, but you can substitute with kale if you prefer a stronger flavor. Start with a smaller amount of kale if you're new to green shakes.
- **Sweetness:** Adjust the sweetness with honey or maple syrup according to your taste preference. The pear will also contribute natural sweetness.
- **Milk:** Use your preferred milk to achieve the desired consistency.

Enjoy your refreshing Pear Spinach Shake!

Creamy Zucchini Shake

Ingredients:

- 1 small zucchini, peeled and chopped (about 1 cup)
- 1/2 cup Greek yogurt or non-dairy yogurt
- 1/2 cup milk of your choice (dairy, almond, soy, etc.)
- 1 ripe banana
- 1 tablespoon honey or maple syrup (or to taste)
- 1/2 teaspoon vanilla extract (optional, for added flavor)
- 1/4 teaspoon ground cinnamon (optional, for extra warmth)
- 1/2 cup ice cubes (optional, for a colder, thicker shake)

Instructions:

1. **Prepare Zucchini:**
   - Peel and chop the zucchini into small pieces. If you prefer a warmer shake, you can use raw zucchini, but if you want a smoother texture, you can steam or blanch the zucchini first and let it cool.
2. **Blend Ingredients:**
   - In a blender, combine the chopped zucchini, Greek yogurt, milk, banana, honey or maple syrup, and vanilla extract (if using).
3. **Blend Until Smooth:**
   - Blend on high until the mixture is smooth and creamy. The zucchini should blend into a smooth texture, providing a creamy base for the shake.
4. **Add Cinnamon (Optional):**
   - For added warmth and flavor, blend in 1/4 teaspoon of ground cinnamon.
5. **Add Ice (Optional):**
   - If you're using fresh zucchini and prefer a thicker, colder shake, add a handful of ice cubes and blend again until smooth.
6. **Serve:**
   - Pour the shake into a glass.
7. **Enjoy:**
   - Serve immediately for a creamy and nutritious treat!

Tips:

- **Zucchini:** Using raw zucchini is fine, but steaming or blanching it beforehand can make it even creamier and easier to blend.
- **Banana:** Adds natural sweetness and creaminess to the shake. Make sure the banana is ripe for the best flavor.
- **Sweetness:** Adjust the sweetness with honey or maple syrup according to your taste.
- **Milk:** Choose any milk you prefer to achieve the desired consistency.

Enjoy your refreshing and creamy Zucchini Shake!

Butternut Squash Shake

Ingredients:

- 1 cup cooked butternut squash (peeled and cubed; steamed or roasted)
- 1/2 cup Greek yogurt or non-dairy yogurt
- 1/2 cup milk of your choice (dairy, almond, soy, etc.)
- 1 ripe banana
- 1 tablespoon honey or maple syrup (or to taste)
- 1/2 teaspoon vanilla extract (optional, for added flavor)
- 1/4 teaspoon ground cinnamon
- 1/4 teaspoon ground nutmeg (optional, for extra warmth)
- 1/2 cup ice cubes (optional, for a colder, thicker shake)

Instructions:

1. **Prepare Butternut Squash:**
   - If not using pre-cooked squash, peel, seed, and cube the butternut squash. Steam or roast the cubes until tender, then let them cool. For roasting, toss the cubes with a bit of olive oil and roast at 400°F (200°C) for about 25-30 minutes.
2. **Blend Ingredients:**
   - In a blender, combine the cooked butternut squash, Greek yogurt, milk, banana, honey or maple syrup, vanilla extract (if using), ground cinnamon, and ground nutmeg (if using).
3. **Blend Until Smooth:**
   - Blend on high until the mixture is smooth and creamy. The butternut squash will give the shake a rich, creamy texture.
4. **Add Ice (Optional):**
   - If you're using fresh butternut squash and prefer a thicker, colder shake, add a handful of ice cubes and blend again until smooth.
5. **Serve:**
   - Pour the shake into a glass.
6. **Enjoy:**
   - Serve immediately for a warm and comforting treat!

Tips:

- **Butternut Squash:** Ensure the squash is fully cooked and tender for the best texture. You can use pre-cooked or frozen butternut squash for convenience.
- **Banana:** Adds natural sweetness and creaminess. Make sure it's ripe for the best flavor.
- **Spices:** Adjust the spices to your taste. Cinnamon and nutmeg complement the sweetness of the butternut squash beautifully.
- **Sweetness:** Adjust with honey or maple syrup according to your preference.

Enjoy your comforting and creamy Butternut Squash Shake!

Spicy Carrot Shake

Ingredients:

- 1 cup fresh or frozen carrot juice
- 1/2 cup Greek yogurt or non-dairy yogurt
- 1/2 cup milk of your choice (dairy, almond, soy, etc.)
- 1 ripe banana
- 1/2 teaspoon ground ginger (or 1/2 tablespoon fresh ginger, peeled and grated)
- 1/4 teaspoon ground cinnamon
- 1/4 teaspoon ground turmeric (optional, for extra warmth and health benefits)
- 1 tablespoon honey or maple syrup (or to taste)
- 1/4 teaspoon cayenne pepper (optional, for a kick of heat)
- 1/2 cup ice cubes (optional, for a colder, thicker shake)

Instructions:

1. **Prepare Ingredients:**
   - If you're using fresh carrots, juice them to get 1 cup of carrot juice. Alternatively, you can use pre-packaged carrot juice. If using fresh ginger, peel and grate it.
2. **Blend Ingredients:**
   - In a blender, combine the carrot juice, Greek yogurt, milk, banana, ground ginger, ground cinnamon, ground turmeric (if using), and honey or maple syrup. Add cayenne pepper if you want a spicy kick.
3. **Blend Until Smooth:**
   - Blend on high until the mixture is smooth and creamy. The banana will add natural sweetness and creaminess to the shake.
4. **Add Ice (Optional):**
   - If you prefer a thicker, colder shake and you're using fresh carrot juice, add a handful of ice cubes and blend again until smooth.
5. **Serve:**
   - Pour the shake into a glass.
6. **Enjoy:**
   - Serve immediately for a spicy and refreshing treat!

Tips:

- **Carrot Juice:** Freshly juiced carrots will give you the most flavor, but pre-packaged carrot juice works well too.
- **Spices:** Adjust the amount of ground ginger, cinnamon, turmeric, and cayenne pepper based on your taste preferences. The spices complement the sweetness of the carrots.
- **Sweetness:** Adjust with honey or maple syrup according to your taste.

Enjoy your spicy and invigorating Carrot Shake!

Vegan Creamy Mushroom Shake

Ingredients:

- 1 cup cooked mushrooms (button, cremini, or your choice)
- 1/2 cup coconut milk or other non-dairy milk
- 1/2 cup unsweetened almond milk (or more, depending on desired consistency)
- 1/2 cup cashews, soaked in water for at least 2 hours (or use pre-soaked cashew butter)
- 1 small garlic clove, minced
- 1 tablespoon nutritional yeast (for a cheesy, umami flavor)
- 1 tablespoon lemon juice
- 1/2 teaspoon dried thyme or rosemary (optional, for extra flavor)
- Salt and pepper, to taste
- 1/4 teaspoon smoked paprika (optional, for a hint of smokiness)
- 1/2 cup ice cubes (optional, for a colder, thicker shake)

Instructions:

1. **Prepare Mushrooms:**
    - If not already cooked, sauté the mushrooms in a pan with a little olive oil until they are tender and browned. Allow them to cool slightly.
2. **Prepare Cashews:**
    - If using raw cashews, soak them in water for at least 2 hours to soften. Drain and rinse before using.
3. **Blend Ingredients:**
    - In a blender, combine the cooked mushrooms, coconut milk, almond milk, soaked cashews, minced garlic, nutritional yeast, lemon juice, dried thyme or rosemary (if using), salt, pepper, and smoked paprika (if using).
4. **Blend Until Smooth:**
    - Blend on high until the mixture is completely smooth and creamy. The cashews will help achieve a rich, creamy texture.
5. **Add Ice (Optional):**
    - If you prefer a colder, thicker shake, add a handful of ice cubes and blend again until smooth.
6. **Serve:**
    - Pour the shake into a glass.
7. **Enjoy:**
    - Serve immediately for a savory and creamy treat!

Tips:

- **Mushrooms:** Use any variety of mushrooms you like. Cooking them first enhances their flavor and makes them easier to blend.

- **Cashews:** Soaking cashews helps create a creamy texture. If you're short on time, you can use cashew butter as a substitute.
- **Seasoning:** Adjust the salt, pepper, and additional spices to suit your taste. Nutritional yeast adds a cheesy flavor, enhancing the umami taste.
- **Consistency:** Adjust the amount of almond milk to achieve your desired consistency.

Enjoy your savory and creamy Vegan Mushroom Shake!

Chocolate Peanut Butter Milkshake

Ingredients:

- 2 cups vanilla ice cream (or a non-dairy alternative for a vegan option)
- 1/2 cup milk of your choice (dairy or non-dairy)
- 1/4 cup creamy peanut butter
- 1/4 cup chocolate syrup (or 2 tablespoons cocoa powder with 2 tablespoons honey or maple syrup)
- 1/2 teaspoon vanilla extract (optional, for added flavor)
- Whipped cream (optional, for topping)
- Chocolate shavings or chopped peanuts (optional, for garnish)

Instructions:

1. **Blend Ingredients:**
   - In a blender, combine the vanilla ice cream, milk, creamy peanut butter, chocolate syrup (or cocoa powder and sweetener), and vanilla extract (if using).
2. **Blend Until Smooth:**
   - Blend on high until the mixture is smooth and creamy. The ice cream and milk will create a rich, creamy base, while the peanut butter and chocolate syrup will add flavor.
3. **Serve:**
   - Pour the milkshake into a tall glass.
4. **Garnish (Optional):**
   - Top with whipped cream and garnish with chocolate shavings or chopped peanuts, if desired.
5. **Enjoy:**
   - Serve immediately with a straw or a spoon for a delicious treat!

Tips:

- **Consistency:** Adjust the amount of milk to achieve your desired thickness. For a thicker shake, use less milk or more ice cream.
- **Peanut Butter:** Use creamy peanut butter for a smooth texture, but you can use chunky peanut butter if you prefer some texture.
- **Chocolate Syrup:** If using cocoa powder, adjust the sweetness to taste. You can increase the amount of honey or maple syrup if needed.

Enjoy your indulgent and creamy Chocolate Peanut Butter Milkshake!

Vanilla Almond Protein Shake

Ingredients:

- 1 cup almond milk (or milk of your choice)
- 1 scoop vanilla protein powder (whey or plant-based)
- 1/4 cup almond butter (or 2 tablespoons of almond meal)
- 1/2 teaspoon vanilla extract
- 1 ripe banana
- 1 tablespoon honey or maple syrup (optional, for added sweetness)
- 1/4 teaspoon ground cinnamon (optional, for added warmth)
- 1/2 cup ice cubes (optional, for a colder, thicker shake)

Instructions:

1. **Prepare Ingredients:**
   - If using a whole banana, peel and slice it. If using almond butter, ensure it's smooth and well-stirred.
2. **Blend Ingredients:**
   - In a blender, combine the almond milk, vanilla protein powder, almond butter, vanilla extract, banana, honey or maple syrup (if using), and ground cinnamon (if using).
3. **Blend Until Smooth:**
   - Blend on high until the mixture is completely smooth and creamy. The banana will add natural sweetness and creaminess.
4. **Add Ice (Optional):**
   - If you prefer a thicker, colder shake, add a handful of ice cubes and blend again until smooth.
5. **Serve:**
   - Pour the shake into a glass.
6. **Enjoy:**
   - Serve immediately for a refreshing and protein-packed treat!

Tips:

- **Protein Powder:** Choose a high-quality vanilla protein powder that suits your dietary preferences (whey, pea, hemp, etc.).
- **Almond Butter:** If you prefer, you can use almond meal instead of almond butter for a different texture.
- **Sweetness:** Adjust the sweetness with honey or maple syrup according to your taste. The banana also contributes natural sweetness.
- **Consistency:** Adjust the amount of almond milk to achieve your preferred thickness.

Enjoy your nourishing and flavorful Vanilla Almond Protein Shake!

Berry Oatmeal Shake

Ingredients:

- 1 cup mixed berries (fresh or frozen; strawberries, blueberries, raspberries, etc.)
- 1/2 cup rolled oats
- 1/2 cup Greek yogurt or non-dairy yogurt
- 1/2 cup milk of your choice (dairy, almond, soy, etc.)
- 1 tablespoon honey or maple syrup (or to taste)
- 1/2 teaspoon vanilla extract (optional, for added flavor)
- 1/2 teaspoon ground flaxseed or chia seeds (optional, for added nutrition)
- 1/2 cup ice cubes (optional, for a colder, thicker shake)

Instructions:

1. **Prepare Oats:**
   - If you prefer, you can soak the oats in milk or water for about 10 minutes to soften them, but this step is optional.
2. **Blend Ingredients:**
   - In a blender, combine the mixed berries, rolled oats, Greek yogurt, milk, honey or maple syrup, and vanilla extract (if using).
3. **Blend Until Smooth:**
   - Blend on high until the mixture is smooth and creamy. The oats will blend into the shake, adding a nice texture and creaminess.
4. **Add Ice (Optional):**
   - For a thicker, colder shake, add a handful of ice cubes and blend again until smooth.
5. **Add Flaxseed or Chia Seeds (Optional):**
   - For extra nutrition, blend in 1/2 teaspoon of ground flaxseed or chia seeds.
6. **Serve:**
   - Pour the shake into a glass.
7. **Enjoy:**
   - Serve immediately for a refreshing and filling treat!

Tips:

- **Berries:** Use a mix of your favorite berries. Frozen berries work well if you want a thicker shake and colder temperature.
- **Oats:** Rolled oats are best for blending. If you prefer a smoother texture, you can use quick oats or oat flour.
- **Sweetness:** Adjust the sweetness with honey or maple syrup according to your taste. The berries will add natural sweetness.
- **Consistency:** Adjust the amount of milk to achieve your desired thickness.

Enjoy your delicious and wholesome Berry Oatmeal Shake!

Pineapple Coconut Shake

Ingredients:

- 1 cup fresh or frozen pineapple chunks
- 1/2 cup coconut milk (full-fat or light, depending on your preference)
- 1/2 cup Greek yogurt or non-dairy yogurt
- 1/2 cup milk of your choice (dairy or non-dairy)
- 1 tablespoon honey or maple syrup (or to taste)
- 1/2 teaspoon vanilla extract (optional, for added flavor)
- 1/4 cup shredded coconut (optional, for added texture)
- 1/2 cup ice cubes (optional, for a colder, thicker shake)

Instructions:

1. **Prepare Ingredients:**
    - If using fresh pineapple, peel and chop it into chunks. If using frozen pineapple, you can add it directly to the blender.
2. **Blend Ingredients:**
    - In a blender, combine the pineapple chunks, coconut milk, Greek yogurt, milk, honey or maple syrup, and vanilla extract (if using).
3. **Blend Until Smooth:**
    - Blend on high until the mixture is smooth and creamy. The pineapple and coconut will blend into a rich, tropical shake.
4. **Add Shredded Coconut (Optional):**
    - For added texture and a more intense coconut flavor, blend in 1/4 cup of shredded coconut.
5. **Add Ice (Optional):**
    - If you prefer a thicker, colder shake, add a handful of ice cubes and blend again until smooth.
6. **Serve:**
    - Pour the shake into a glass.
7. **Enjoy:**
    - Serve immediately for a refreshing and tropical treat!

Tips:

- **Pineapple:** Use fresh pineapple for a vibrant flavor, or frozen pineapple for a thicker, colder shake.
- **Coconut Milk:** Choose the type of coconut milk based on how rich and creamy you want the shake to be. Full-fat coconut milk will make it richer, while light coconut milk will be less creamy.
- **Sweetness:** Adjust the sweetness with honey or maple syrup according to your taste. Pineapple is naturally sweet but you can add more sweetener if needed.

- **Consistency:** Adjust the amount of milk and ice to achieve your desired consistency.

Enjoy your tropical Pineapple Coconut Shake!

Kale Pineapple Shake

Ingredients:

- 1 cup fresh kale leaves (stems removed)
- 1 cup fresh or frozen pineapple chunks
- 1/2 cup Greek yogurt or non-dairy yogurt
- 1/2 cup coconut water or plain water
- 1/2 cup milk of your choice (dairy or non-dairy)
- 1 tablespoon honey or maple syrup (or to taste)
- 1/2 teaspoon vanilla extract (optional, for added flavor)
- 1/2 cup ice cubes (optional, for a colder, thicker shake)

Instructions:

1. **Prepare Ingredients:**
   - Wash and remove the stems from the kale leaves. If using fresh pineapple, peel and chop it into chunks. If using frozen pineapple, you can add it directly to the blender.
2. **Blend Ingredients:**
   - In a blender, combine the kale leaves, pineapple chunks, Greek yogurt, coconut water or plain water, milk, honey or maple syrup, and vanilla extract (if using).
3. **Blend Until Smooth:**
   - Blend on high until the mixture is smooth and creamy. The kale will blend into the shake, adding nutrients without overpowering the flavor.
4. **Add Ice (Optional):**
   - For a thicker, colder shake, add a handful of ice cubes and blend again until smooth.
5. **Serve:**
   - Pour the shake into a glass.
6. **Enjoy:**
   - Serve immediately for a refreshing and nutritious treat!

Tips:

- **Kale:** Using fresh kale will provide the best texture and flavor. If you're new to kale, start with a small amount and increase as you get accustomed to the taste.
- **Pineapple:** Fresh pineapple adds a bright flavor, but frozen pineapple will make the shake thicker and colder.
- **Sweetness:** Adjust the sweetness with honey or maple syrup according to your taste. Pineapple is naturally sweet, but you might want to add more sweetener if needed.
- **Consistency:** Adjust the amount of coconut water or milk to achieve your desired consistency.

Enjoy your invigorating Kale Pineapple Shake!

Apple Cinnamon Shake

Ingredients:

- 1 large apple (peeled, cored, and chopped)
- 1/2 cup Greek yogurt or non-dairy yogurt
- 1/2 cup milk of your choice (dairy or non-dairy)
- 1/4 cup apple juice or apple cider
- 1 tablespoon honey or maple syrup (or to taste)
- 1/2 teaspoon ground cinnamon
- 1/4 teaspoon vanilla extract (optional, for added flavor)
- 1/2 cup ice cubes (optional, for a colder, thicker shake)

Instructions:

1. **Prepare Ingredients:**
    - Peel, core, and chop the apple into small pieces. If you prefer, you can briefly cook the apple pieces in a pan with a little water to soften them, but this step is optional.
2. **Blend Ingredients:**
    - In a blender, combine the chopped apple, Greek yogurt, milk, apple juice or cider, honey or maple syrup, ground cinnamon, and vanilla extract (if using).
3. **Blend Until Smooth:**
    - Blend on high until the mixture is smooth and creamy. The apple and yogurt will blend together to create a rich and flavorful shake.
4. **Add Ice (Optional):**
    - For a colder, thicker shake, add a handful of ice cubes and blend again until smooth.
5. **Serve:**
    - Pour the shake into a glass.
6. **Enjoy:**
    - Serve immediately for a deliciously comforting treat!

Tips:

- **Apple:** Use any variety of apple you prefer. A sweet apple like Fuji or Honeycrisp works well, but you can use tart apples for a different flavor.
- **Sweetness:** Adjust the sweetness with honey or maple syrup according to your taste. The apple juice or cider adds natural sweetness.
- **Cinnamon:** If you like a stronger cinnamon flavor, feel free to adjust the amount to your preference.

Enjoy your cozy and flavorful Apple Cinnamon Shake!

Sweet Potato Pie Shake

Ingredients:

- 1 cup cooked sweet potato (peeled and cubed; can be fresh or canned)
- 1/2 cup Greek yogurt or non-dairy yogurt
- 1/2 cup milk of your choice (dairy or non-dairy)
- 1/4 cup maple syrup or honey (adjust to taste)
- 1/2 teaspoon ground cinnamon
- 1/4 teaspoon ground nutmeg
- 1/4 teaspoon vanilla extract
- 1/4 teaspoon ground ginger (optional, for extra spice)
- 1/2 cup ice cubes (optional, for a colder, thicker shake)

Instructions:

1. **Prepare Sweet Potato:**
    - If using fresh sweet potato, peel and cube it, then cook until tender (you can steam, boil, or bake it). If using canned sweet potato, make sure it's plain (not sweetened or spiced).
2. **Blend Ingredients:**
    - In a blender, combine the cooked sweet potato, Greek yogurt, milk, maple syrup or honey, ground cinnamon, ground nutmeg, vanilla extract, and ground ginger (if using).
3. **Blend Until Smooth:**
    - Blend on high until the mixture is smooth and creamy. The sweet potato will blend into the shake, creating a rich texture and flavor.
4. **Add Ice (Optional):**
    - For a thicker, colder shake, add a handful of ice cubes and blend again until smooth.
5. **Serve:**
    - Pour the shake into a glass.
6. **Enjoy:**
    - Serve immediately for a deliciously comforting treat!

Tips:

- **Sweet Potato:** Use cooked sweet potato for the best texture. If using canned, make sure it's just sweet potato with no added sugars or spices.
- **Sweetener:** Adjust the sweetness with maple syrup or honey according to your taste preference. The shake can be made sweeter or less sweet based on your preference.
- **Spices:** Adjust the spices to your taste. You can add more cinnamon or nutmeg if you like a spicier flavor.

Enjoy your creamy and flavorful Sweet Potato Pie Shake!

Greek Yogurt Pancake Batter Shake

Ingredients:

- 1 cup Greek yogurt (plain or vanilla)
- 1/2 cup milk of your choice (dairy or non-dairy)
- 1/2 cup rolled oats
- 1/4 cup maple syrup or honey (adjust to taste)
- 1/2 teaspoon vanilla extract
- 1/2 teaspoon ground cinnamon
- 1/4 teaspoon baking powder (optional, for a fluffier texture)
- 1/4 cup ice cubes (optional, for a colder, thicker shake)

Instructions:

1. **Prepare Ingredients:**
   - Measure out all ingredients. If you prefer, you can briefly soak the oats in a little bit of milk for a few minutes to soften them, but this step is optional.
2. **Blend Ingredients:**
   - In a blender, combine the Greek yogurt, milk, rolled oats, maple syrup or honey, vanilla extract, ground cinnamon, and baking powder (if using).
3. **Blend Until Smooth:**
   - Blend on high until the mixture is smooth and creamy. The oats will blend in and help thicken the shake, giving it a texture reminiscent of pancake batter.
4. **Add Ice (Optional):**
   - For a thicker, colder shake, add a handful of ice cubes and blend again until smooth.
5. **Serve:**
   - Pour the shake into a glass.
6. **Enjoy:**
   - Serve immediately for a delicious and nutritious treat!

Tips:

- **Greek Yogurt:** Use plain or vanilla Greek yogurt for a rich, creamy base. If you prefer a tangier taste, plain yogurt works well.
- **Sweetener:** Adjust the sweetness with maple syrup or honey according to your taste. You can also use other sweeteners like agave or stevia if preferred.
- **Consistency:** Adjust the amount of milk to achieve your desired thickness. For a thinner shake, add more milk.

Enjoy your delightful Greek Yogurt Pancake Batter Shake!

Easy Blender Salsa Shake

Ingredients:

- 1 cup salsa (mild, medium, or hot, depending on your preference)
- 1/2 cup Greek yogurt (plain or non-dairy yogurt)
- 1/4 cup milk of your choice (dairy or non-dairy)
- 1/2 avocado (for creaminess)
- 1/2 cup ice cubes (optional, for a colder, thicker shake)
- Fresh cilantro (optional, for garnish)

Instructions:

1. **Prepare Ingredients:**
   - Measure out the salsa, Greek yogurt, milk, and avocado. If you prefer a cooler shake, you can add ice cubes.
2. **Blend Ingredients:**
   - In a blender, combine the salsa, Greek yogurt, milk, and avocado.
3. **Blend Until Smooth:**
   - Blend on high until the mixture is smooth and creamy. The avocado adds a creamy texture, while the salsa provides a fresh, tangy flavor.
4. **Add Ice (Optional):**
   - For a colder, thicker shake, add a handful of ice cubes and blend again until smooth.
5. **Serve:**
   - Pour the shake into a glass.
6. **Garnish (Optional):**
   - Garnish with fresh cilantro if desired.
7. **Enjoy:**
   - Serve immediately for a unique and flavorful treat!

Tips:

- **Salsa:** Choose a salsa that you enjoy eating on its own. The flavor of the salsa will be prominent in the shake.
- **Avocado:** The avocado adds creaminess and a subtle richness to the shake. If you want a less creamy shake, you can reduce the amount of avocado or leave it out.
- **Milk:** Adjust the amount of milk to achieve your desired consistency. For a thicker shake, use less milk.

Enjoy your adventurous and savory Easy Blender Salsa Shake!

Roasted Tomato Sauce Shake

Ingredients:

- 1 cup roasted tomato sauce (homemade or store-bought; ensure it's not too chunky)
- 1/2 cup Greek yogurt (plain or non-dairy yogurt)
- 1/2 cup milk of your choice (dairy or non-dairy)
- 1/4 cup cooked and cooled quinoa or rice (for added texture)
- 1/2 teaspoon dried basil or oregano (optional, for extra flavor)
- 1/4 teaspoon garlic powder (optional, for added depth)
- 1/4 teaspoon onion powder (optional, for added depth)
- Fresh basil or parsley (optional, for garnish)
- 1/2 cup ice cubes (optional, for a colder, thicker shake)

Instructions:

1. **Prepare Ingredients:**
   - Measure out the roasted tomato sauce, Greek yogurt, milk, and cooked quinoa or rice. If you prefer a colder shake, prepare ice cubes.
2. **Blend Ingredients:**
   - In a blender, combine the roasted tomato sauce, Greek yogurt, milk, quinoa or rice, dried basil or oregano (if using), garlic powder (if using), and onion powder (if using).
3. **Blend Until Smooth:**
   - Blend on high until the mixture is smooth and creamy. The quinoa or rice adds a slightly grainy texture and makes the shake more substantial.
4. **Add Ice (Optional):**
   - For a colder, thicker shake, add a handful of ice cubes and blend again until smooth.
5. **Serve:**
   - Pour the shake into a glass.
6. **Garnish (Optional):**
   - Garnish with fresh basil or parsley if desired.
7. **Enjoy:**
   - Serve immediately for a savory and comforting treat!

Tips:

- **Tomato Sauce:** Use a high-quality roasted tomato sauce for the best flavor. If the sauce is too chunky, you might want to blend it first to smooth it out.
- **Quinoa/Rice:** The cooked quinoa or rice adds body to the shake. You can adjust the amount based on how thick you want the shake to be.
- **Spices:** Adjust the spices to your taste. You can add more dried herbs or spices if you like a stronger flavor.

Enjoy your savory and unique Roasted Tomato Sauce Shake!

www.ingramcontent.com/pod-product-compliance
Lightning Source LLC
LaVergne TN
LVHW081616060526
838201LV00054B/2279